Finding Employment as an Older Adult

Tips and Strategies

Ruth Smith

A. Smith Media

CONTENTS

INTRODUCTION

The job market can be challenging for anyone, but it can be particularly difficult for older adults who may face ageism and a lack of opportunities for part-time or flexible work. However, with the right strategies and a positive attitude, it is possible for older adults to find fulfilling and rewarding employment. This book will discuss some tips and strategies for finding a job when you are retired or above 55 years of age. We will also explore the benefits of part-time and freelance work, the importance of continuing education and training, and the role of networking and making connections. By following these tips and strategies, older adults can increase their chances of success in the job market.

CHAPTER 1

THE CHALLENGES OF FINDING A JOB AS AN OLDER ADULT.

As individuals age, finding a job can become increasingly difficult. Older adults often face unique challenges in the job market, including age discrimination, outdated skills, and a lack of flexibility in the workplace.

One of the major challenges faced by older adults is age discrimination. Despite being illegal, many employers still have unconscious biases against hiring older workers. This can lead to older adults being passed over for job opportunities, even if they are well-qualified and experienced.

Additionally, older adults may struggle to keep their skills up to date in a rapidly changing job market. With technology advancing at a rapid pace, older workers may find that their skills are no longer in demand or that they need to learn new skills to remain competitive. This can be a daunting task, especially for those who have been out of the job market for an extended period of time.

Finally, older adults may face challenges in the workplace itself. Many employers expect their employees to be available for long hours and frequent travel, which can be difficult for older adults who may have family or health obligations. This lack of flexibility can make it difficult for older adults to find a job that fits their needs and lifestyle.

Finding a job as an older adult can be a challenging and daunting task. However, with determination and persistence, older adults can overcome these challenges and find fulfilling and rewarding employment.

CHAPTER 2

THE BENEFITS OF PART-TIME AND FREELANCE WORK FOR OLDER WORKERS.

For older workers, part-time and freelance work can provide a number of benefits.

First, these types of work arrangements can offer flexibility and control over one's schedule. Older workers may have other commitments, such as caring for grandchildren or maintaining a healthy lifestyle, and part-time and freelance work can allow them to balance these responsibilities.

Second, part-time and freelance work can provide opportunities for older workers to continue working and contributing to the economy, even if they are no longer able to work full-time. This can help to maintain their sense of purpose and fulfillment, and can also provide a source of income.

Third, part-time and freelance work can allow older workers to continue developing their skills and expertise. Many older workers have a wealth of experience and knowledge, and part-time and freelance work can provide opportunities to continue using and growing these skills.

Part-time and freelance work can be a great option for older workers looking for flexibility, control, and continued opportunities for growth and development.

CHAPTER 3

STRATEGIES FOR HIGHLIGHTING YOUR SKILLS AND EXPERIENCE.

For older workers, highlighting their skills and experience is crucial to maintaining a competitive edge in the job market. As they approach retirement age, many older workers may feel their skills and experience are not as valuable as younger workers, but this is not the case.

One strategy for highlighting your skills and experience as an older worker is to focus on your transferable skills. These are skills that can be applied to various industries and job positions, such as communication, problem-solving, and leadership. Emphasizing these skills can show employers that you are adaptable and versatile, and can bring value to their organization.

Another strategy is to showcase your experience and accomplishments. Highlight your past successes, particularly those that demonstrate your ability to take on new challenges and deliver results. Be sure to include any awards, certifications, or special training you have received, as these can all serve as evidence of your expertise.

In addition, consider networking with other professionals in your industry. Networking can help you stay up-to-date on industry trends and opportunities, and can also provide valuable connections to potential employers. Attend industry events, join professional organizations, and connect with others on LinkedIn to expand your network and showcase your skills and experience.

Finally, consider updating your resume and LinkedIn profile to highlight your skills and experience. Use keywords and phrases that are relevant to your industry, and focus on the skills and experience that make you stand out. You may also want to include a summary or objective statement that summarizes your value proposition and showcases your expertise.

By focusing on your transferable skills, showcasing your experience and accomplishments, networking with others in your industry, and updating your resume and LinkedIn profile, you can effectively highlight your skills and experience as an older worker and remain competitive in the job market.

CHAPTER 4

NETWORKING AND MAKING CONNECTIONS TO FIND JOB OPPORTUNITIES.

Networking and making connections are crucial for finding job opportunities for older workers. As people age, they may face discrimination in the job market and face difficulty in finding employment. However, networking and making connections can open up new job opportunities and allow older workers to showcase their skills and experiences.

Networking can involve attending job fairs, joining professional organizations, and attending industry events. These events allow older workers to meet potential employers and learn about job opportunities. Additionally, networking can involve reaching out to friends, family, and former colleagues for job leads and referrals.

Making connections is also important for finding job opportunities for older workers. Older workers can leverage their existing connections to find job opportunities and get introductions to potential employers. Additionally, older workers can make connections through social media, such as LinkedIn, to expand their network and learn about job opportunities.

In addition to networking and making connections, older workers can also utilize job search websites and job boards to find job opportunities. Many of these websites and job boards have specific sections for older workers and can provide access to job listings that may not be readily available through networking and connections.

Networking and making connections are key for finding job opportunities for older workers. By leveraging these strategies, older workers can showcase their skills and experiences and gain access to job opportunities that may not be readily available through traditional job search methods.

CHAPTER 5

THE IMPORTANCE OF BEING OPEN TO NEW OPPORTUNITIES.

As people get older, their opportunities for career advancement and growth may seem to dwindle. But it is important for older workers to remain open to new opportunities, as they can provide valuable experiences and benefits.

One of the main advantages of being open to new opportunities is that it can lead to career growth and advancement. Even if an older worker feels like they have reached a plateau in their current job, taking on a new role or responsibility can help them to develop new skills and knowledge. This can open up new doors and opportunities for promotion or advancement within their current organization or in a new one.

Additionally, being open to new opportunities can help older workers to remain engaged and motivated in their careers. Taking on new challenges and responsibilities can provide a sense of purpose and meaning, which can be particularly important as people get older and may be facing retirement.

Furthermore, being open to new opportunities can also provide financial benefits. Older workers may be able to negotiate higher salaries or better benefits when taking on a new role, which can help to improve their financial security in the long term.

It is important for older workers to remain open to new opportunities, as they can provide valuable experiences, career growth, and financial benefits. By remaining open and flexible, older workers can continue to thrive and make a valuable contribution to their organizations and communities.

CHAPTER 6

TIPS FOR UPDATING YOUR RESUME AND COVER LETTER FOR A JOB SEARCH.

As an older worker, it can sometimes be difficult to stand out in the job market. Your experience and skills may be just as valuable as younger candidates, but it can be challenging to effectively communicate that to potential employers. By updating your resume and cover letter, you can increase your chances of standing out and landing the job you want.

1. Tailor your resume and cover letter to the specific job you are applying for. This means highlighting your experience and skills that are most relevant to the position. For example, if you are applying for a management position, focus on your leadership experience and ability to manage teams.

2. Use action verbs to describe your accomplishments and experiences. This will help to make your resume more engaging and show employers that you are a capable and accomplished worker. For example, instead of saying "managed a team," you could say "led a team of 10 employees to achieve a 10% increase in sales."

3. Include any additional training or certifications you have acquired since your last job search. This will show employers that you are committed to staying current in your field and are willing to invest in your own

professional development.

4. Highlight any achievements or accolades you have received in your previous positions. This will help to show potential employers that you are a top performer and can bring value to their organization.

5. Keep your resume and cover letter concise and to the point. Avoid using overly long sentences or jargon, as this can make your writing difficult to understand. Focus on highlighting your most relevant experience and skills, and be sure to proofread your documents for errors.

By following these tips, you can update your resume and cover letter to effectively communicate your value as an older worker in the job market. By highlighting your experience and skills, and tailoring your documents to the specific job you are applying for, you can increase your chances of standing out and landing the job you want.

CHAPTER 7

HOW TO ADDRESS AGEISM IN THE JOB MARKET.

Ageism in the job market is a pervasive issue that affects older workers. This discrimination based on age often leads to older individuals being passed over for job opportunities, despite their experience and qualifications.

To address ageism in the job market, it is important to first raise awareness about the issue. Many people may not realize that ageism exists and the impact it has on older workers. This can be done through educational campaigns and workshops, as well as through discussions with employers and job seekers.

Another key step in addressing ageism is to implement policies and practices that protect older workers from discrimination. This can include instituting age-based hiring quotas or providing training for managers on how to avoid ageist bias.

Additionally, older workers can take steps to counteract ageism by highlighting their experience and qualifications in their job applications and interviews. This can include highlighting skills and experience that are relevant to the job, and showing how they can bring value to the organization.

Overall, addressing ageism in the job market for older workers requires a combination of education, policy changes, and individual action. By working together, we can create a more inclusive and fair job market for older workers.

CHAPTER 8

THE ROLE OF TECHNOLOGY IN HELPING OLDER ADULTS FIND JOBS.

In recent years, technology has played a vital role in helping older adults find jobs. With the rise of the internet and social media, older workers are able to access a wider range of job opportunities than ever before.

One of the key ways in which technology helps older adults find jobs is through online job search platforms. These platforms allow older workers to easily search for job openings that match their skills and experience. Many of these platforms also have tools that allow users to tailor their resumes and cover letters to specific job openings, which can be particularly helpful for older workers who may not have extensive experience with online job applications.

Social media platforms, such as LinkedIn, are also useful tools for older adults looking for jobs. These platforms allow users to connect with potential employers and showcase their skills and experience. In addition, older workers can use social media to network with other professionals in their field, which can help them learn about job opportunities that may not be advertised elsewhere.

Another key benefit of technology for older workers is the ability to work remotely. Many older adults may not be able to commute long distances to work, but with the rise of remote work, they are able to find jobs that allow them to work from home. This can be particularly helpful for older workers who may have physical limitations or other challenges that make it difficult to work in a traditional office setting.

Technology has played a crucial role in helping older adults find jobs. With the help of online job search platforms, social media, and remote work opportunities, older workers are able to access a wider range of job opportunities and showcase their skills and experience to potential employers. As technology continues to evolve, it is likely that older workers will continue to benefit from its ability to connect them with job opportunities.

CHAPTER 9

THE BENEFITS OF CONTINUING EDUCATION AND TRAINING FOR OLDER WORKERS.

As people age and approach retirement, they may be tempted to slow down and focus on enjoying their golden years. However, continuing education and training can have numerous benefits for older workers.

First and foremost, continuing education and training can help older workers stay competitive in the job market. With advancements in technology and changes in industry standards, older workers may find that their skills and knowledge are no longer sufficient to meet the demands of their current job or to find new employment. By staying up to date with the latest developments in their field, older workers can remain valuable to their employers and increase their chances of securing new job opportunities.

Continuing education and training can also help older workers increase their earning potential. By acquiring new skills and knowledge, older workers can take on more complex tasks and responsibilities, which can lead to promotions and higher salaries. Furthermore, older workers who continue to learn and grow can demonstrate their dedication and adaptability to their employers, which can make them more attractive to potential employers.

In addition to the financial benefits, continuing education and training can also have numerous personal and professional benefits for older workers. For example, continuing education and training can help older workers stay engaged and motivated in their work, which can lead to increased job satisfaction and a better overall quality of life. It can also provide older workers with a sense of accomplishment and personal growth, which can boost their self-esteem and confidence.

Furthermore, continuing education and training can help older workers maintain their mental and physical health. By engaging in stimulating activities, older workers can keep their minds sharp and prevent cognitive decline. Additionally, many forms of continuing education and training, such as fitness classes or workshops on healthy eating, can help older workers maintain a healthy lifestyle and prevent chronic diseases.

Continuing education and training can have numerous benefits for older workers. It can help them stay competitive in the job market, increase their earning potential, and provide personal and professional benefits. By investing in their own growth and development, older workers can continue to thrive and enjoy their later years.

CHAPTER 10

THE VALUE OF INTERNSHIPS AND VOLUNTEERING FOR OLDER JOB SEEKERS.

Internships and volunteering can be incredibly valuable for older job seekers, especially those who may be returning to the workforce after a period of absence or are looking to change careers. These opportunities offer a way for older workers to gain hands-on experience and build their skills, while also networking and making connections in their field.

One of the biggest benefits of internships and volunteering for older job seekers is the opportunity to learn new skills and stay current in their industry. Many older workers may have years of experience in their field, but the constantly changing nature of the job market means that they may need to update their skills in order to remain competitive. Internships and volunteering provide a chance for older workers to learn new technologies and techniques, as well as stay abreast of industry trends and developments.

Additionally, internships and volunteering can provide valuable networking opportunities for older job seekers. These experiences allow older workers to make connections with potential employers, as well as other professionals in their field. This can be especially useful for those who are looking to change careers, as they can gain insight and advice from those who have already made the transition.

Another important benefit of internships and volunteering for older job seekers is the opportunity to gain experience and build a resume. Many employers are looking for candidates with relevant experience, and internships and volunteering can provide older workers with the chance to add to their resume and demonstrate their skills and abilities. This can be especially important for those who may have gaps in their employment history or are looking to change careers.

Internships and volunteering can be incredibly valuable for older job seekers. These opportunities offer a way for older workers to gain hands-on experience, learn new skills, and make connections in their field. By taking advantage of internships and volunteering, older workers can remain competitive in the job market and increase their chances of finding fulfilling and meaningful employment.

CHAPTER 11

THE IMPACT OF THE GIG ECONOMY ON JOB OPPORTUNITIES FOR OLDER WORKERS.

The gig economy has had a significant impact on job opportunities for older workers. The gig economy, also known as the sharing economy, is a labor market characterized by the prevalence of short-term contracts or freelance work as opposed to permanent jobs.

One of the main advantages of the gig economy for older workers is that it provides flexible work opportunities. Many older workers prefer to work part-time or on a flexible schedule, and the gig economy allows them to do so. This flexibility can be particularly beneficial for older workers who may have health or family caregiving responsibilities.

However, the gig economy also has its drawbacks for older workers. Gig work is often precarious, with low pay and few or no benefits. This can make it difficult for older workers to earn a stable income and save for retirement. Gig work may also be physically demanding, which can be challenging for older workers who may have age-related health issues.

Furthermore, the gig economy has led to an increase in competition for jobs. Older workers may face age discrimination in the gig economy, as employers may prefer younger workers who are perceived to be more adaptable and technologically savvy.

The gig economy has both advantages and disadvantages for older workers. While it provides flexible work opportunities, it can also be precarious and competitive. It is important for policymakers and employers to address these challenges and ensure that older workers are able to access decent and stable work in the gig economy.

CHAPTER 12

HOW TO USE SOCIAL MEDIA TO FIND JOB OPPORTUNITIES.

Social media is a valuable tool for older workers seeking job opportunities. With the rise of online platforms, it has become easier for job seekers to connect with potential employers and showcase their skills and experience.

To effectively use social media for job hunting, older workers should start by creating a professional online profile that highlights their qualifications, experience, and achievements. This should include a clear, updated resume, a professional headshot, and relevant keywords to help recruiters find them.

Next, they should actively engage with industry professionals and organizations on social media. This can be done by joining relevant LinkedIn groups, following industry leaders and companies on Twitter and Instagram, and participating in discussions and sharing relevant content. This helps to build a network and gain visibility within the industry.

Older workers should also utilize job search tools on social media platforms, such as LinkedIn's job search function and Twitter's job listings. These tools allow them to search for job opportunities based on their location, industry, and experience level, making it easier to find the right fit.

Additionally, older workers can use social media to showcase their skills and experience by creating a portfolio on platforms such as LinkedIn, showcasing their past projects and achievements. This allows them to showcase their expertise and capabilities to potential employers, increasing their chances of being considered for job opportunities.

Social media is a valuable tool for older workers seeking job opportunities. By creating a professional online profile, actively engaging with industry professionals and organizations, utilizing job search tools, and showcasing their skills and experience, older workers can effectively use social media to find job opportunities.

CHAPTER 13

THE ROLE OF PROFESSIONAL ORGANIZATIONS AND SUPPORT GROUPS FOR OLDER JOB SEEKERS.

Professional organizations and support groups play a crucial role in helping older job seekers navigate the job market and find employment. These organizations provide a wide range of resources and support services that can help older job seekers stay competitive and increase their chances of finding a job.

One of the key benefits of professional organizations and support groups for older job seekers is the access they provide to networking opportunities. These organizations often host networking events and job fairs where older job seekers can connect with potential employers and other job seekers. They can also provide access to job listings and job search resources that can help older job seekers find job opportunities that align with their skills and experience.

Professional organizations and support groups can also help older job seekers stay up-to-date on industry trends and developments. These organizations often offer workshops, seminars, and other training programs that can help older job seekers develop new skills and stay current in their field. This can be particularly important for older job seekers who may need to update their skills or knowledge to stay competitive in the job market.

In addition to providing access to resources and training,

professional organizations and support groups can also offer emotional support and guidance to older job seekers. These organizations often have support groups or mentoring programs that can help older job seekers cope with the challenges of job searching and provide them with the encouragement and support they need to keep going.

Overall, professional organizations and support groups play a crucial role in helping older job seekers find employment and succeed in their careers. By providing access to networking opportunities, training, and support, these organizations can help older job seekers stay competitive and increase their chances of finding a job that aligns with their skills and experience.

CHAPTER 14

THE IMPORTANCE OF A POSITIVE ATTITUDE IN A JOB SEARCH.

As we age, the job search process can become more challenging. Older job seekers may face ageism and stereotypes, and may have a harder time competing with younger, more technologically savvy candidates. In these circumstances, a positive attitude can make all the difference.

A positive attitude allows older job seekers to approach their search with confidence and optimism. It helps them to focus on their strengths and achievements, rather than dwelling on potential obstacles or setbacks. A positive attitude can also make a good impression on potential employers, who may be more likely to hire someone who is enthusiastic and confident.

Furthermore, a positive attitude can help older job seekers to stay resilient and motivated during the job search process. It can help them to persevere through rejection and disappointment, and to keep trying until they find a job that is right for them.

In addition, a positive attitude can help older job seekers to stay open-minded and adaptable. It can encourage them to explore new opportunities and consider different career paths, rather than limiting themselves to the same jobs they have always done. A positive attitude can also help them to learn new skills and technologies, which can make them more competitive in the job market.

A positive attitude is essential for older job seekers who want to succeed in their job search. It can give them the confidence, resilience, and adaptability they need to overcome the challenges they may face, and to find a fulfilling and rewarding job.

CHAPTER 15

STRATEGIES FOR NEGOTIATING SALARY AND BENEFITS AS AN OLDER WORKER.

As an older worker, negotiating salary and benefits can be a daunting task. However, there are strategies that can help you get the compensation you deserve.

First, do your research. Know the average salary and benefits for your position and industry in your area. This will give you a benchmark to negotiate from.

Next, highlight your experience and expertise. Older workers often bring a wealth of knowledge and skills to the table, and it's important to showcase these when negotiating.

Third, focus on the value you will bring to the company. Discuss the specific ways you can contribute to the organization's success and how your experience will benefit the team.

Fourth, be willing to compromise. While it's important to negotiate for what you want, be open to alternative benefits or other forms of compensation. For example, if the company is unable to offer a higher salary, they may be able to offer additional vacation time or professional development opportunities.

Finally, be confident and assertive. Don't be afraid to advocate for yourself and your worth. Trust in your abilities and don't settle for less than you deserve.

Negotiating salary and benefits as an older worker requires

research, highlighting your value, being open to compromise, and confidence in your abilities. By using these strategies, you can secure the compensation you deserve.

CHAPTER 16

THE BENEFITS OF STARTING A BUSINESS OR CONSULTANCY IN RETIREMENT.

Retirement is often seen as a time to relax and enjoy the fruits of one's labor. However, for many older workers, starting a business or consultancy in retirement can provide a number of benefits.

One of the biggest advantages of starting a business or consultancy in retirement is the opportunity to continue using one's skills and expertise. Older workers often have decades of experience in their field, and starting a business or consultancy allows them to put this experience to use in a new and exciting way. This can be particularly fulfilling for those who have spent their careers in a particular industry and want to continue contributing to it in some way.

Another benefit of starting a business or consultancy in retirement is the potential for additional income. Many older workers are on a fixed income, and starting a business or consultancy can provide a source of supplemental income that can help to boost their retirement savings and improve their financial security. This can be particularly important for those who are looking to maintain their current standard of living in retirement.

In addition to the potential for additional income, starting a business or consultancy in retirement can also provide a sense of purpose and fulfillment. Many older workers find that they miss the challenges and rewards of working in their field, and starting a business or consultancy can provide a way to continue engaging with their chosen industry in a meaningful way. This can be particularly beneficial for those who are looking to maintain their mental and emotional well-being in retirement.

Starting a business or consultancy in retirement can provide a number of benefits for older workers. Whether they are looking to continue using their skills and expertise, generate additional income, or find a sense of purpose and fulfillment, starting a business or consultancy can be a great way to make the most of their retirement years.

CHAPTER 17

THE IMPACT OF RETIREMENT SAVINGS AND PENSIONS ON JOB OPPORTUNITIES.

The impact of retirement savings and pensions on job opportunities as an older worker is significant. As workers approach retirement age, they often begin to focus on saving for their retirement and building a pension. This can have a number of consequences for their job opportunities.

First, as workers focus on building their retirement savings and pensions, they may be less likely to take on new job opportunities or promotions that require them to work longer hours or take on additional responsibilities. This can limit their options as they approach retirement, making it more difficult to find a new job or to advance in their current career.

Second, employers may be less likely to offer job opportunities to older workers who are focused on building their retirement savings and pensions. This is because employers may view these workers as less committed to their jobs and less likely to stay with the company long-term. As a result, older workers may face discrimination in the job market, making it harder for them to find employment.

Third, retirement savings and pensions can also impact job opportunities for older workers in a more positive way. For example, workers who have built up a significant amount of retirement savings and have a solid pension may be able to afford to retire earlier than other workers. This can open up job opportunities for younger workers who are looking to enter the workforce or advance in their careers.

The impact of retirement savings and pensions on job opportunities as an older worker is complex and can have both positive and negative effects. While these savings and pensions can provide security and stability in retirement, they can also limit job opportunities and cause discrimination in the job market.

CHAPTER 18

THE ROLE OF GOVERNMENT PROGRAMS AND RESOURCES IN HELPING OLDER WORKERS FIND JOBS.

As an older worker, finding a job can be a challenging task. Many employers may view older workers as less productive or less adaptable to new technologies and job duties. However, government programs and resources can play a significant role in helping older workers find employment.

One way the government can help is through job training and education programs. These programs can provide older workers with the skills and knowledge necessary to adapt to changing job markets and industries. For example, the Department of Labor's Senior Community Service Employment Program (SCSEP) offers job training and job placement services for individuals over the age of 55 who are unemployed or underemployed.

Another way the government can help is by providing financial assistance to older workers. The Social Security Administration offers a program called the "Retirement Earnings Test," which allows individuals to earn a certain amount of money from employment without it affecting their Social Security benefits. This program can provide financial support to older workers who may be hesitant to return to the workforce due to concerns about losing their benefits.

In addition, the government can also provide resources and

support for older workers who are self-employed or starting their own businesses. The Small Business Administration offers a variety of programs and services specifically designed for older entrepreneurs, such as business counseling, training, and access to capital.

Government programs and resources can play a crucial role in helping older workers find employment. By providing job training, financial assistance, and support for entrepreneurship, the government can help older workers adapt to changing job markets and continue to contribute to the economy.

CHAPTER 19

THE IMPORTANCE OF HEALTH AND WELLNESS IN MAINTAINING A SUCCESSFUL CAREER AT ANY AGE.

Maintaining good health and wellness is crucial for a successful career at any age. This is because good health and wellness allows individuals to stay physically and mentally fit, which is necessary for them to perform their job duties efficiently and effectively.

Good health and wellness also enables individuals to handle stress and challenges at work effectively. Stress can take a toll on an individual's physical and mental health, leading to burnout and decreased productivity. By maintaining good health and wellness, individuals can manage stress and other challenges at work without letting them affect their performance.

In addition, good health and wellness can also increase an individual's confidence and motivation. When individuals feel good about themselves and their health, they are more likely to approach their work with enthusiasm and determination. This can lead to better performance and increased job satisfaction.

Furthermore, good health and wellness can also improve an individual's relationships with their coworkers and supervisors. When individuals are in good health, they are more likely to be positive and energetic, which can foster good working relationships and better collaboration.

The importance of health and wellness in maintaining a successful career at any age cannot be overemphasized. By prioritizing their health and wellness, individuals can stay physically and mentally fit, manage stress, improve their confidence and motivation, and foster good working relationships.

CHAPTER 20

THE POTENTIAL OF REMOTE WORK AND FLEXIBLE SCHEDULES FOR OLDER WORKERS.

The potential of remote work and flexible schedules for older workers has the potential to greatly benefit both the workers and their employers. For older workers, remote work and flexible schedules offer the opportunity to continue working and earning a living while maintaining a work-life balance that accommodates their changing needs and priorities.

Remote work allows older workers to work from home or other locations outside of the traditional office setting, allowing them to avoid the physical demands and time constraints of commuting. Flexible schedules allow them to adjust their work hours to fit their personal schedules and preferences, allowing them to prioritize their health and well-being.

For employers, offering remote work and flexible schedules to older workers can result in increased productivity, job satisfaction, and retention of valuable employees. Older workers often bring a wealth of experience and knowledge to the workplace, and offering them the ability to work remotely and on a flexible schedule can help them stay engaged and motivated.

In addition, remote work and flexible schedules can also benefit older workers by providing them with access to a wider range of job opportunities. Many older workers may be unable or unwilling to relocate for work, and remote work and flexible schedules can provide them with the opportunity to work for companies located outside of their immediate area.

The potential of remote work and flexible schedules for older workers is significant. By offering these options, employers can provide older workers with the flexibility and support they need to continue working and contributing to the workforce. In turn, older workers can enjoy the benefits of continued employment and a better work-life balance, ultimately leading to a more productive and satisfying work experience.

CONCLUSION

In conclusion, the topics discussed above in this book highlight the challenges and opportunities that older adults face in the job market. Finding a job when you are over 55 can be challenging, but it is possible. By focusing on your skills and experience, networking and making connections, and being open to new opportunities, you can increase your chances of finding a fulfilling and rewarding job. Additionally, taking advantage of resources such as part-time and freelance work, continuing education and training, and government programs can help you navigate the job market and find success in your career at any age.

ABOUT THE AUTHOR

Ruth Smith

Ruth Smith is a seasoned professional with over 40 years of experience in the workforce. She has a strong background in management and leadership, and has worked in a variety of industries including finance, healthcare, and education.

Ruth has a particular interest in the potential of remote work and flexible schedules for older workers. She believes that these options can provide older workers with the support they need to continue working and contributing to the workforce, while also allowing them to prioritize their health and well-being.

Ruth is passionate about advocating for the rights of older workers and helping them to achieve a successful and satisfying work experience. She regularly writes about this topic and has been featured in various industry publications.

In her free time, Ruth enjoys spending time with her family, traveling, and volunteering for various organizations in her community.